SURGICAL RAPE

Medical Abuse

A TRUE STORY BY

MzAnn

AuthorHouse™
1663 Liberty Drive
Bloomington, IN 47403
www.authorhouse.com
Phone: 1 (800) 839-8640

Published by AuthorHouse 05/19/2018

ISBN: 978-1-5462-3924-6 (sc)
ISBN: 978-1-5462-3923-9 (e)
Library of Congress Control Number: 2018905040

Print information available on the last page.

Any people depicted in stock imagery provided by Getty Images are models,
and such images are being used for illustrative purposes only.
Certain stock imagery © Getty Images.

This book is printed on acid-free paper.

Scripture quotations marked KJV are from the Holy Bible, King James Version (Authorized Version). First published in
1611. Quoted from the KJV Classic Reference Bible, Copyright © 1983 by The Zondervan Corporation.

authorHOUSE®

CONTENTS

PREFACE...iv

AUTHOR'S DISCLAIMER OF HATRED FOR ENEMY.................................vii

DEDICATIONS viii

FYI, DOS AND DON'TS IN SEEKING MEDICAL/LEGAL ADVICE 1

COMPLAINT LETTER TO HOSPITAL INVOLVED 3

DEAR READERS, PLEASE FEEL MY PAIN!!! 9

MOTHER'S ENDLESS NIGHTMARE! 11

MY PERSONAL FEELINGS 21

WHY REOPEN THIS CASE? 23

DEFINITIONS/MEDICAL/LEGAL TERMS 26

UNLAWFUL ACTIONS BY ATTORNEY 30

CASES/ORGANIZATIONS THAT FIGHTS FOR JUSTICE 32

POST REMARKS 33

ABOUT THE AUTHOR...35

LEGAL REFERENCES PROVIDED IN THIS BOOK 36

ENTERTAINING POEMS..37

HOW TO BECOME A CHRISTIAN... 44

PREFACE

IN LIGHT OF STATISTICS AFFIRMING that medical malpractice cases which end up in court shows only 21% in favor of the patient is sufficient proof that doctors get awarded the undeserved victory crowns. The one who inflicted the injury gets a pat on the back and goes on to the next victim! Therefore, all Americans should fight along with me to amend that unconstitutional law! If that edit remains as it stands, then anyone or your loved one could be the next unsuspecting victim. So, it is for that reason that I, an innocent victim compiled this little information booklet. I wrote this with much prayer that my unjust court case would be reconsidered as soon as possible. But this time with all of my injuries laid bare to the court. This serious issue should not have been merely about whether or not my doctor breached the Standard of Care, which that was all the court was afforded the opportunity to hear. My attorney had let me down by misrepresenting me before the court. The only issue my attorney saw fit to prove in that 3-day proceeding, was did the doctor step outside of the standard of care in his surgical techniques. Neither did my attorney see fit to make the hospital responsible for breaking the law along with my doctor.

Additionally, even the jury was rigged against me in that one juror flat out said he was against a doctor ever being sued. After that juror made that bias statement he should have been disqualified beforehand. And all the people on the defendant's team appeared to be close friends, even upwards, to the judge. Thus, in this informative booklet I chose to withhold the names of those but true names will be revealed whenever the new trial is granted. Thanks be to God from 2010 until now, I still have the court transcripts. But, for now my doctor is simply Doctor X. And my attorney is simply nameless.

This brief story was created from notes I had jotted down over the years as I was angrily ventilating the injustice. And I am yet hurting nowadays, here in 2018. I am still in tears and very, very disgusted that I had received absolutely no justice regarding the inhumane act inflicted upon my body way back in that 2005 surgery. The case did not get to court until five years after the surgery. Then after I lost that case, in disbelief, the numerous times I sat jotting down notes, I also wondered how was it that my surgeon, who apparently had sworn under the Hippocratic Oath, feel that it was anyway just to sit there in court and bold-faced lie! As I stared across the room into his eyes, it was obvious he hadn't an ounce of guilt about leaving me to suffer the consequences of his surgical abuse. Nor did he feel any remorse about his breach of the **Standard of Care** towards me in spite of what his lying lawyer was defending him against! (See S.O.C on definitions page). I was also appalled at how Dr. X could literally scheme along with his attorney to cheat me out of all of my healthy organs without any restitution! How was it that he made such a humongous mistake and then got clear away with it in a civil court of American law, in 2010? (see definitions).

And here is the "kicker" that has been so difficult for me to forget! During that single surgery he mistakenly removed my healthy kidney, a healthy adrenal gland and a healthy spleen. However, before Doctor X had begun to perform his part of the surgery, the OB/GYN, who had been scheduled to do a total hysterectomy had finished. Then, Doctor X proceeded to remove all of the above healthy organs in that one single surgical procedure! So, I wonder where was the **common sense** of two skilled doctors not making a decision not to gut the patient in one procedure!? How did this mistake happen in that, Dr. X, himself, according to court transcript, had dictated that he was to perform a splenectomy? Then during the surgery, he nor the OB-GYN had recognized that the other organs Dr. X were removing were a kidney along with the adrenal gland. How could Doctor X, after handling a normal size kidney with his very own skilled hands still not identify it was a kidney rather than an adrenal mass as he affirmed he thought the kidney was a mass? Nevertheless, the pathologist, after having received the normal-sized kidney in her lab, had identified it as a kidney. Then, according to the court transcript she directly after receiving the kidney, called Dr. X and informed him that he had labeled the container's contents as an Adrenal Mass rather than the actual Kidney and Adrenal gland it acrually contained. (Breach of the Standard of Care. See definition). And from that day until now I am always ill and has been declared disabled. And, no, I was not ill before the surgery other than PMS just like so many other females. As a result, even now my spirit remains restless over this unrighteous attack on my body while I lay there helpless! So, I cannot help but to feel as though I was robbed of my healthy organs while under the influence of drugs, so **Surgical Rape is exactly what I call it!!**

Thus, I've decided to write this booklet to expose those careless doctors and crooked lawyers. No one should have to suffer neither physically nor mentally the way I am continuing to bare. While Dr. X, The Surgical Specialists, Doctor X's insurance company and that Hospital have chosen to ignore this serious matter, I am still in pain right this day as I write this booklet. So that with this information others may heed the warning to beware of negligent doctors and dishonest lawyers. Also, for people to beware of attorneys who is the only defender in his law firm. Rather you should please, please seek attorneys who has affiliation with a group of capable lawyers! And also get a third opinion about your medical diagnosis because Dr. X was only my second opinion. Sadly, I find it necessary to reiterate that the single attorney I hired had no other honest lawyers to discipline his deception. So, I learned the hard way but now am compelled to warn other would be victims to be more vigilant of the tricks of the devil. Sadly, I've learned that the smell of money has the ability to dull integrity! And another thing, I cannot claim that race was a motivator for my losing the case, because Dr. X and I are the same race. Nevertheless, I can and will claim that him being rich and me being poor was for sure, the major factor in me losing the case. I can also claim that it was our social difference that put the stone in his sling, because during the 3-day trial my attorney, the older lawyer I actually had hired, finally tried his hand at defending me. He reluctantly brought up my poverty status. (the older attorney had hired the younger attorney who did the talking in court). When the older attorney tried to interject my social state, the attorney for the defense objected and said that social status should not be brought into this case. **So, it is my prayer that an honest attorney will read this booklet and contact me with help with both a medical and legal malpractice suit. Because every other attorney I have asked to take this case have admitted that they do not sue other lawyers.** So, in the face of those flat-out rejections, how will I ever obtain the justice I deserve? But, thank God I have a heavenly Attorney and Judge, my Father! And, one more thing readers should know. Just because I am not laid in a bed, you might think I'm as fit as a fiddle. But I refuse to quit pushing on a daily basis just to keep my body from buckling. Not all that shines are gold, sometimes it can be fool's gold. You might see me and think "Oh, she's fine, nothing is wrong with her!"

AUTHOR'S DISCLAIMER OF HATRED FOR ENEMY

Forgiveness

(Romans 12:14-21) KJV

¹⁴Bless them which persecute you: bless, and curse not. ¹⁵Rejoice with them that do rejoice, and weep with them that weep. ¹⁶*Be* of the same mind one toward another. Mind not high things but condescend to men of low estate. Be not wise in your own conceits. ¹⁷Recompense to no man evil for evil. Provide things honest in the sight of all men. ¹⁸If it be possible, as much as Leith in you, live peaceably with all men. ¹⁹Dearly beloved, avenge not yourselves, but *rather* give place unto wrath: for it is written, Vengeance *is* mine; I will repay, saith the Lord. ²⁰Therefore if thine enemy hunger, feed him; if he thirst, give him drink: for in so doing thou shalt heap coals of fire on his head. ²¹Be not overcome of evil, but overcome evil with good.

If my enemies were hungry, I would certainly feed them and thirsty, I would give them water. I do not hate the people who wronged me, but rather, for justice is all I plead!

DEDICATIONS

THANKS TO MY PRECIOUS, ALL knowing, Heavenly Father, who knew this time would come for me to tell my story. I'm so abundantly grateful for the strength Father, that you've given me to push through the tears, fears, heartaches and physical pain. Lord, it was you who held me together. Father I couldn't have completed this book without you. You have been my shelter in the times of storm. I'm truly blessed! THANK YOU!!!

Thanks to my Dear Mother who has been a rock of stability throughout my life, especially with this ordeal. You are the strongest woman I know! Though you have your own burdens to bare you never gave up on helping me. Your sacrifice, time and dedication are much appreciated. I'm truly blessed to have a Christian mom such as you! Thanks again Momz!

To my dear, adorably sweet son (Mijo) who has shown me that no matter what life throws your way, there is always a solution to the problem, (Just Google It), lol. Son you have grown into a beautiful strong young man. Never let this life take away what God has blessed you with, continue to follow your dreams but most of all, follow Christ. I thank God for watching over you!

To my Aunt Char, thanks for your listening ear. Anytime I was feeling a little under the weather, you were always there to give me a godly-word of encouragement. I thank God for such a sweet Aunt such as you.

All of my aunts have been so helpful in different phases of my life, starting with Aunt Frankie during my childhood, even when she had many mouths to feed she always had enough for me too, and my Aunt Barbara who at one point opened her home to me. I will always remember such nice gestures.

Thanks to all of my wonderful cousins. I know we don't spend as much time as we use to as kids but the beauty is we will spend much more time in Heaven together one day. I love each one of you. Thanks again for all the support throughout the years and for the beautiful necklace. I wear it close to my heart and each stone represents each one of you.

And to the ministers of the West End Church of Christ. Doctor, Brother Orpheus J. Heyward and Brother Adam McGill. Brother Orpheus has been a God-sent servant to our congregation. We all glorify the Lord that he gave Brother O the gift of teaching others how to rightly divide the word in this religiously confused generation! And Brother Adam is such a good and patient servant for all of us. He really studies to show himself approved unto God. And our leadership is the best heaven has to offer! And one of God's shepherds, Brother Wm. Johnson, may God bless you for sticking with me through this stormy time!

Finally, thanks to you readers for taking the time to read this booklet. God Bless you!

FYI, DOS AND DON'TS IN SEEKING MEDICAL/LEGAL ADVICE

DO:

- Whenever a doctor too quickly suggest surgery is the best route, **do** question that.
- Whenever a doctor uses medical terminology you do not understand, **do** write it down for research. Have the doctor spell the word.
- Whenever a doctor seems to want to schedule surgery before the year is over, **do** ask why is surgery so urgent and does your life depend on the speedy surgery?
- Whenever a doctor tells you that you have a certain growth or mass, either inside or outside of your body and doctor do not see fit to run a battery of tests, **do** ask how dangerous the illness is, and insist he run tests first.
- Again, whenever a doctor seems too speedy with an exam then advises you that surgery may be the best cure, **do** question that.
- Whenever a doctor has performed tests and advises you that you need surgery, **do** get a second and third opinion, maybe even a fourth.
- Whenever a doctor refuses to allow a family member into the exam room with you, **do** let that be your last visit to that office.
- Whenever a doctor or assistant will not let you know what your vital signs were during that visit, **do** ask and let doctor know you would prefer to be informed each time.
- Whenever a doctor run tests or perform surgery, **do** request that your Personal Care Physician (PCP) is sent a copy directly from the surgeon's office.
- **Do** make sure that you hire a reputable law firm, good standing with the Bar Association.

- **Do** make sure you complete an American background check on the owner of the firm.
- **Do** ask if they take cases on a contingency basis. (They get paid when you get paid).
- **Do** be prepared with all the information about what happened between you and the surgeon and the hospital in which you were injured.
- **Do** write down any questions you may have for the attorney.
- **Do** make sure you are able to understand his dialect if he has one. Communication is key.
- **Do** take note of how he/she react to your lack of understanding of the law. You are a lay-person and not expected to know the law.
- **Do** be suspicious if he wants to know if you have a family member who is an attorney.

DON'T

- **DON'T** hire one single attorney... **very important** that you hire a law firm of several attorneys.
- **Don't** allow the Stature of Limitation on medical malpractice to expire (not one day past two years after the accident). See definitions.
- **Don't** be too shy to ask how long doctor or attorney has been practicing.
- **Don't** be too quick to judge the attorney's skin color. Race should not be a major factor, credential should.
- **Don't** hire attorney or doctor until you have done a thorough American background check.
- **Don't** sign any papers until you or an attorney have an understanding what you are signing. Once a doctor takes out your organs, that's final!
- **Don't** forget to make a list of questions for each visit to doctor or attorney.
- **DON'T** pay any fees except for consultation fees, if applicable.
- **DON'T** be afraid to fire attorney if they refuse to explain more clearly when advising you.
- **DON'T** miss any appointments if possible.
- **DON'T** allow attorney to have only one Expert Witness on your behalf... The more doctors on you team, the better chance you have of winning.

COMPLAINT LETTER TO HOSPITAL INVOLVED

A **FEW YEARS AFTER I** had lost the unfair court battle and in a desperate attempt to achieve some kind of fairness I sent the following letter to the **Board of Trustees at the Hospital:**

To Whom It May Concern:

This communication is to inform you that your establishment made a grave mistake during my surgery in 2005. One of the physicians, Dr. X, from Surgical Specialists had used your facility to perform my surgery where he removed several healthy organs, the major one being a kidney.

Then shortly after the surgery the hospital pathologist had called the operating room and informed Dr. X that a normal-size kidney which she had not expected to be receiving in the first place, was put into the container and labeled, Adrenal Mass. I feel that Dr. X's first wrong move was that he had not informed me the patient beforehand that I was to have an adrenal mass nor a kidney removed. But rather he had prior informed me that I had **a mass abutting against the Spleen and that he was positive I needed to have a splenectomy only**. Which now I know that he even misinformed me of needing my spleen removed in that small lesions are common in the spleen. I have medical records to prove what we had discussed regarding only the splenectomy. Also, during my recovery Dr. X had come to my room and said, "Ms. Morman I apologize, but I had to remove your kidney because it was too small". I replied by saying "God already knew the outcome". In a daze and not able to digest what I was hearing, that was my way of having faith that God was still in control.

I went on to write in this letter to the Hospital: The reason I am bringing this incident to your attention at this late date is because there is a legal system called, "Discovery" and since I now know that your hospital should have been named in the law suit which I filed in 2007. However, my Attorney had failed to represent me accordingly as my defender. Additionally, your facility at that time also failed to inform me that Dr. X had made that horrific mistake. He had violated the Standard of Care (readers, see definitions page). Instead all of you had seen fit to keep quite knowing that this doctor removed heathy organs and also labeled the container incorrectly. So, I ask, how was it that your pathologist was able to identify the organs but Dr. X and his associate was not able to? Even after Dr. X cut away the adrenal gland he still should have been able to identify the attached organ as a kidney. But your pathologist was able to identify the organ attached to the adrenal gland was indeed a kidney. It is evident that every surgeon should know the human anatomy before finishing school and being allowed to perform life threating surgeries. Where is the trustworthiness to your patient on behalf of your Hospital? I now still suffer with several severe health problems that I did not have in the past. You can find proof by my growing stack of medical records that I am now very ill! Also, check the numerous visits I've had to your Clinic since that surgery. I was even seen there by Dr. Z, who I believe is the Chief Director at the Hospital Clinic. I recall speaking to him one day about my many medical ailments and prior healthy history. As he and I had conversed one day, I brought up Dr. X's name. One thing that stood out was that through our conversation Dr. Z had directly defended Dr. X. and completely dismissed my feelings and the physical anguish I was in at that time and am still suffering. Doctor Z went on to say that Dr. X had performed surgery on a family member of his and that Dr. X did a great job. I simply sat there feeling how that statement had been very bias and indifference when it was clear that I had come to him suffering both physically and mentally, expecting pity if nothing else. Nevertheless, he did prescribe an antidepressant. See Dr. Z's notes, I had suggested in the letter. In his notes he had readily defended Dr. X. It seemed as though this doctor did not agree with me and had difficulty believing that Dr. X was capable of making such damaging mistakes.

In the letter I continued to say, Additionally, as a result of the surgery, I had to visit a mental therapist because going through all of that I had begun to have anxiety attacks. Then after speaking to the therapist she told me something that I would never have expected was possible. She had informed me that I was subconsciously grieving the loss of those organs as one would over the loss of a child at birth. And her telling me that made sense and put some things into perspective about my mental stress. Because, even before I had that visit with her, I felt the need to call my ex-attorney and ask him what had the hospital done with my kidney, my baby. Now I realize I was in a grieving process at that time but did not know it. All I knew was that there were dots I just was unable to connect as a lay-person and victim! And, your hospital being "Secret Holders" what about the pain and suffering I'm still encountering, even as I write this letter? Because, as a child and young adult I was never a sickly person until Dr. X removed all those healthy vital organs, all at once! Having removed that many organs all at one time has literally propelled my body into a shock-frenzy causing me to have puss filled breakouts all over my body. Plus, I was married at the time and my husband was afraid to touch me with those ugly boils. Of course, I could not blame him because no one had explained to us what I would go through after having so many healthy organs mistakenly removed. Dr. X gave me one shot and that was a pneumococcal. I found out later that he should have administered a battery of preventive shots since he was the one who almost took my life! And so far, my spirit remains restless over this inhumane attack on my body. I feel as though someone raped me while I was under the influence of drugs. Surgical Rape is what I call it! So, I'm writing an informative booklet and will soon publish it because no one should suffer the physical and mental abuse the way I am still suffering while Dr. X, Surgical Specialists and Your Hospital simply have ignored this serious matter that's still hurting as I write.

I have also developed several chronic medical problems including Sjogren's, an Autoimmune Disorder. And I could not believe it when I was diagnosed with Rheumatoid Arthritis! Now why would such a young woman as I suddenly develop RA. And I have never even heard the word, Sjogren's! Now I realize, for sure, my quality of life has been taken away! And, to boot, with this kind of disability I've been forced to live in public housing, not of my own choosing but because I can no longer maintain a job. I'm having to constantly visit one doctor after another with various ailments. I guess I will never adjust to being a sickly person. At the tender age of early 4os

I feel like 70's. The last time I really knew myself as a healthy woman was when I was having only female issues just as thousands of women naturally does. Even now this disability affords a very limited amount of quality life.

Below is a list of medical conditions I struggle with on a daily basis. **However, I had none of these illnesses before that botched surgery.** Now, I suffer all the time and **Social Security is footing the bill. That measly SSDI have to take care of a disability that should have been generously compensated by Dr. X, Surgical Specialist and your Hospital. I have thought seriously about appealing to the Social Security Administration about who should really be responsible for my disability.** Then maybe the SS office could enquire as to why they are paying insurance benefits instead of those responsible parties. Because Dr. X and his lying lawyer lied before the Court System, and before the Almighty God by claiming that **Dr. X removed my organs because he suspected angio-sarcoma.** I have court transcripts where my Expert Witness testified that Dr. X, nor any doctor, have absolutely no right to remove a healthy organ. There had been no sane reason for his action and I still say, **"There had been sheer madness behind his cutting frenzy that day"**. Could it be that he was angry at someone and took it out on me! And, now as I lay awake nights, I find myself wondering if it was another case of **Black-Market, boot-leg?** Another thing that bothers me is why Dr. X had openly **lied about suspecting angio-sarcoma?** Why had he not brought in an oncologist before he started removing those healthy organs? **Or he could have sent over a tissue sample for a frozen section to the pathologist if he truly suspected cancer.** And why was I not told when he came to my recovery room of his medical suspicion? Why did he not tell my mother who was in the waiting room, about this suspicion of cancer? And my husband was also only a phone call away.

My mother was only told that he eventually had to remove my kidney. So, Dr. X was aware that he had removed a kidney. So why had he labeled the container as an Adrenal Mass? He deliberately breached the Standard of Care. See definitions. Sounds fishy to me! Plus, my husband should have been told, but instead Dr. X left my family under the same impression, that my Kidney had been infected or something. **He also never told my Primary Care Physician that he suspected Angio-sarcoma nor that he had removed all those**

organs. I also have medical records as proof that Doctor X never talked to my PCP at all, neither before or after the surgery. As a matter of fact, if one were to review his dictations one would not discover any serious claims of him ever suspecting **I had Angio-sarcoma.** There are many doctors that make mistakes but they quickly confess their shortcomings along with a formal apology and some kind of restitution. I also deserve a personal apology from Dr. X, The Surgical and Your Hospital! I had written in the letter that day.

Now I can recall that whenever I am asked by other doctors why so many organs were removed, I tell them that it was because I was told I had a mass that needed removing. I never offer them any other details. That is mainly because in the past whenever I would tell some doctors, they would be astounded over this type of action. Then their next question would be, **"Which hospital did the surgery happen in?"** But, it's strange, how most never asked which doctor performed the surgery. So, back to the letter. . . My friends and family are mad and appalled at what happened and the injustice I have received and are ready to go to Washington with me. Those kind gestures are what keeps me going and of course the strength I always receive from God Almighty! My health is failing fast, but I understand that the body will eventually deteriorate anyway, but as long as God continues to keep my mind healthy and strong I will continue to fight this matter to the end. I am resolved that before I die the world will know about the surgical rape that happened in my small town!

I now ask, "Where is the fiduciary, Standard of Care in Your Hospital once the pathologist had discovered a grave mistake had been made?" Does the Hospital simply leave it up to every physician to be honest? As you can see, not all doctors are trustworthy. And I have transcripts as proof that physicians will lie to patients who have entrusted their lives to them. I trusted Dr. X and now I am greatly suffering the consequences. What hurts most is that **if I were any other race than Black, I would not have to fight this intensely for my rights!** I'm so glad that I have a God who sees the deeds of the good and of the bad. . . **The bad deeds of Dr. X, Surgical Specialist and Your Hospital!**

The bottom line is that I am a poor woman of whom it was convenient to take advantage. So, I have also resolved to pray without ceasing that God will bring this awful injustice to the light of the news media! I have already taken this matter all the way to the US Supreme Court via Pro Se only (a defending appeal method for the poor). So, thank God my mother is a published author! However, I know that God is the final Judge of this great, double malpractice.

In closing I am requesting a meeting with the Directors of Your Hospital to personally express this situation, as soon as possible. Thanks!

DEAR READERS, PLEASE FEEL MY PAIN!!!

IN 2013, EIGHT YEARS AFTER that awful surgery, I had an appointment with a famous Orthopedic Services, one of the many doctor visits I'd had over the years since that horrific surgery. As I waited in the exam room the doctor finally entered and after viewing my chart he playfully said to me that I had had a lot of Ec-tomies. He was right, I'd had a splenectomy, nephrectomy, appendectomy, adrenalectomy and a hysterectomy, all during one surgery. Ashamed and still in pain from that vicious attack on my body, I simply tried to laugh it off but inside I was crying realizing his next question would be, "Why did you have those organs removed?" And he asked just that. My answer was that the surgeon's intentions was to remove my spleen because of a mass abutting from my spleen he saw on the MRI. So, in essence, my surgeon mistakenly removed my healthy left kidney, a healthy spleen and a healthy left adrenal gland. I had expected to have the hysterectomy and a mass removed from my spleen.

So, during my visit that day with the Orthopedic doctor, I went on to tell him that after the surgery was over the Pathology report had shown that all organs removed had been healthy and that there was no mass to be found. In other words, the surgery, with the exception of the hysterectomy, had been unnecessary!!! There in the exam room with the Orthopedic that day I found myself becoming too emotional. So as not to continue with his questions I closed the conversation by simply commenting "Mistakes happen, you know!" Frankly, ever since the surgery I began to view every doctor as a friend of Dr. X. and that they would outright defend him. Readers, can you feel my pain whenever Dr. X is defended by someone?

Still, since that surgery ordeal I have had to turn to mental therapy only to discover that I was unknowingly grieving the loss of those healthy organs. Thus, family and friends are doing as much as they can to keep me from reliving that awful ordeal. Nevertheless, mentally it has been a struggle to forget that suffering since I'm in pain on a daily basis! And sadly, Doctor X has yet to own up to his mistake, only adds fuel to the fire. Absurdly he must be forced to do the right thing. And even though a few other physicians stated that this surgery was unnecessary, I still received no mercy in court. And it is because of Dr. X that I now must receive disability insurance from Social Security. Also, he took away my ability to hold a normal job and now must suffer disgrace by having to reside in subsidized housing. It would be a great relief if only I could get on the media and show the world this story. But, thus far I must continue to suffer and live in silence!! You readers out there please, please feel my pain!!! Is there anyone else out there who has been wronged by a doctor or lawyer the way I have? If so, let's get together and go after those thieving, lying wolves!

MOTHER'S ENDLESS NIGHTMARE!

ALL OF YOU PARENTS OUT there, whether you are the parent of a small child or an adult. When your child hurts there is nothing, except sell your soul, that you would not do to ease their hurt! However, in my daughter's brutal case there was no earthy balm or bandage to reach for like when she was a little girl. All I have been able to do is watch her suffer all these years since that terrible surgery. And to top off her bearing bodily pain, eventually I've had to help bare her mental anguish.

My ill daughter lost the court case in 2010 where Dr. X, the judge, the defending Expert Witnesses (3 doctors) and Dr. X's lawyer all were friends. And during the entire 3-day-circus-of-a-trial they had uncouthly scoffed at my daughter, where I totally lost faith in the American judicial system. Especially when I knew that the lawyer whom her initial lawyer had hired, was also a friend of the opposing team. **We suspected that second lawyer had literally taken a bribe to withhold evidence he had right there in his briefcase. He had deliberately misrepresented her in court. Had he shown pictures of the oozing sores and break-outs on her body to prove that was a reaction from having lost all those healthy organs, there would have been a chance. I know that would have won some damage reparation. So, we can rightfully claim it was all a mean set-up. Because, again, whenever that lawyer had an opportunity to plug in an objection, he chose to remain silent. Now, what aggressively, defending attorney goes through a three-day trial and never once objects to anything the defense says? So, we can boldly claim that he threw that case!** Additionally, when we tried to file a legal malpractice suit, we were told repeatedly by various law firms that lawyers did not sue other lawyers! Those rejections left us feeling we had run head on into another brick wall! So, in light of lawyers refusing to make other lawyers responsible for their deliberate sins, how could we possibly receive justice? And one of those upscale law Firms was one that is known all over the world. Believe me, we will be honored to disclose names when this case is reopened so that they can be exposed for what they are! Then the world will make the righteous judgment, either for the doctor and lawyer, or for my daughter.

Plus, all the medication doctors had prescribed my daughter, with which even a horse should not be that inundated! And with only one kidney and no spleen, if she had consumed that amount of medication over time, surely that kidney would soon fail. I can thank only God that years earlier, He had allowed me to become a registered Histology Tech, where I learned about certain medications. Plus, I still cringe when I think of how Dr. X had gutted my daughter the way he would a fish fresh out of water! First of all, he had removed way too many organs during just a single surgery. And it appeared Dr. X knew which organs not to remove so as not to take her life right then and there. However, one never knows how the Almighty in His providence works things out. Maybe God wanted Dr. X to eventually be caught in his follies in that there is no telling how many patients has been his, human prey. It is a fact that the rich are able to pay any sum for a compatible organ and often does. Nevertheless, we as finite beings might think, "**Well, why did God not stop the surgery or even allowed her some financial restitution in court?**" Then I recall the scripture in Isaiah 55: 8, which says, "My thoughts are not your thoughts" says the Lord, "Neither are My ways your ways!" Maybe this kind of injustice was not for my daughter only. Maybe there are others who will benefit from this scenario whenever it gets to the public.

At times during the appeals, in 2011, I would see a little light at the end of the tunnel. But then, as a mother, my heart would cry out watching my daughter's fading hope whenever we would receive a reply from the court of appeals that our appeal was rejected. That was when we soon discovered that the law is set up for poor people to fail. **B**ecause in 1 Timothy 6: 10, God moved Brother Paul to tell Brother Timothy to remind those greedy saints and all of mankind that, the **love of money** is the root of all evil. Of course, we realize that money is a necessity for mankind to exist, but to **love** it, some would do anything to get more of it the way they did in my daughter's case. But we also know that all un-repented *liars* will take part in the lake that burns with fire and brimstone and they must answer to a Higher Court, Revelation 21: 8. And in Hebrews 9: 27, God's word proves to be powerful and true that it is appointed unto all once to die, and after death comes judgment from Him! Whatsoever we have done in this body will follow us to the after-life. And contrary to popular belief, everyone will be judged sooner or later. And I pray that my daughter's enemies repent and obeys the gospel-call before they are called out of this existence and into the next. By my having said that, is proof I have forgiven my enemies and pray for their souls to be saved. In 2 Thessalonians 2:14, those saints were reminded how every accountable (able to comprehend) soul is called by the gospel that Jesus commanded his hand-chosen Apostles to preach to the world which also reaches to people of today. Even if those who maimed my daughter's body were to apologize to her, they still must make peace with God and be added to His one body, which is His Church of Christ. Acts 2:47, Colossians 1: 18. It is only then can they be saved from the wrath of God when their life on earth is over.

Parents, I know you can identify with me when I tell you how helpless I felt one night when my child called me on the phone in the middle of the night. And knowing her, she would never awaken me if it was not urgent. "Hello," her weak voice a mere whisper. "I'm sorry to awaken you!" now in full tears.

"Oh, that's ok, what's the matter?!" now wide awake for sure. This was before she really learned to be led by the Holy Ghost like she does now. All saints must grow in grace and will be maturing throughout life. "Well," she weakly said as the fretting boils gripped her body, "I wonder if I'm going to know it when they put me into that tiny casket and close the lid?" She'd always had claustrophobia. Then we had to go into prayer and to what the Good Book, in Psalms 116: 15, says, "Precious in the sight of the Lord is the death of His saints". That gave us both faith that God would welcome her with open arms whenever He saw fit to take her home, it would be peaceful and painless. And He has already taken the sting out of death for all of them who are known by Him.

Oh, and back to all the medications that Dr. X and other doctors had prescribed, mainly Statins, Antibiotics and Steroids. She was constantly in search of doctors to explain what was happening to her body. And all they wanted to do was to offer a temporary fix. Statins are for treating high cholesterol, which she surely did not have before the surgery. The steroids, for inflammation, keeps her blown up and antibiotics for infections is bad for the one kidney. Again, before that botched surgery she never had any serious illness that required those strong medications. So, now she was forced to be on medications for the duration of her uncertain life! In the first year after the surgery, she was taking approximately 10 different meds. Then one day when I laid my eyes on that brown paper bag of meds she had carried into the lawyer's office, her son and I, flipped our lid. My first thought was that they were trying to go on and kill her off! For what reason, I really couldn't say. Maybe they knew that she would sooner or later be granted justice and she should have won such a case. So that day as I saw that bag of pills in so many little containers, I demanded that she not take another one. She was already knocking on death's door in that her eyes had become extremely glassy and she consistently complained of having light-headiness and dizziness. So, immediately I went to FATHER in fervent, sincere prayer again to show us a way and to lift our burdens. And He did!! He laid it on my heart to perceive that Dr. X had taken away all of her hormone producing organs. She now had no spleen, which combat infections; no reproduction organs, which she expected to have removed; only one adrenal gland, which puts her at risk of having a stress melt-down and one kidney, which diagnosed her as now having chronic kidney disease. Most of these organs served a specific purpose for the healing process. Isn't that the reason God gives us those organs? During my deep grief and prayers, I feel that God moved me to tell my daughter to go see a Holistic Professional. She lived in the small town at that time and went directly to the **Natural Foods Store**. There, we explained the problem to the professional about my daughter's depleted hormones that by this time, almost two years after the surgery and before the court date, seriously needed replacement. The professional took time and went on a supplement hunt in the store and came back with a 120-count bottle of Gland Tablets for women. These tabs contained all of the essential hormones for females. And thank God after about a week of taking them according to direction her eyes began to look more normal and her light-headiness ceased for the most part. But she has to take those tabs in order to feel normal. And even though we were poor she went on a strict health kick from there, and is doing as well as can be up this day, no thanks to her hospital enemies. I thank God every day for giving my daughter back to me!! She is my only offspring and she also have one son. But then, I always keep in mind that God gave up His only begotten Son to save all of mankind! Alleluia!!!

And another thing I will never forget about that trial. On the second day of the trial, the word, kidney had been mentioned so frequently until when it was time for a break the judge, who had been overly insulting and intimidating to my daughter's attorney before he had agreed sell-out at some point of the trial. Because, in his opening arguments, he had sounded so adamant about getting justice for my daughter. Then, on day 2 he changed from trying so hard to apathy over the proceeding. Not once did he object in a 3-day period. So, back to the judge ordering a break, the judge had jokingly said to the court, "Okay, everyone, let's take a *kidney* break!" and of course, everyone, except my daughter's guests, broke out in laughter. Unfortunate for us the judge had that particular remark struck from the court transcripts. That joke removed her so far from professionalism! And, for sure, she will also get hers along with her partners in crime. Most of these earthly judges should take a long stare into the mirror. It is a fact that they sit so high on their own throne, trying to outshine the throne of God. All I can say to them is, "Beware!" In 1 Corinthians 6: 2, the Holy Spirit says, "Do you not know that you (saints) will judge the world?" The world is a vast sphere and saints can only judge it through God's word. The world is so vast until it encompassed the entire planet of Earth and beyond. All people who live here and take part in these biased laws will be held accountable for disobeying God's righteous rules. Man, simply must do what is right in God's sight and not what is right in our own sight... These judges must rewrite the Justice System Laws that have been darkened for the sake of capital gain. A prime example of this is the case of a high school boy who was found dead, stuffed inside a rolled-up wrestling mat. He had been on the wrestling team at the school where his body was found. His parents were not satisfied with the reason given for their healthy son's death. So, they eventually had his body exhumed for an autopsy. And to everyone's utter shock the boy's insides had all organs missing and had been replaced with newspapers. Now what parent would not be outraged at that discovery of their once healthy, then suddenly dead teenager? And this victim is not the only one on the list who needs his murderers brought to justice!

Last, but certainly not least! Dr. X, while the 3-day trial was in session, carried around a Bible. But, I would like to warn him that the same Book he obviously was reading, would soon become his judge. In Acts 2:38, God commands everyone, "Repent and be baptized every one of you, in the name of Jesus Christ for the remission of sins!" Meaning your past sins would be blotted out by God with the correct teaching and the correct baptism. Thus, during Dr. X 's reading of the Word he so caringly clung to, he must have overlooked that relevant command! Anyone who respect God's word would try wholeheartedly to do the right thing about his surgical mistakes.

So, to my one and only offspring. I have loved you, my Little Girl, ever since I laid eyes on you many years ago. And as your mother, I would gladly give you my organs if I could. However, medical law would prohibit me from sharing a kidney with you because of my age and hypertension status. Though I may not be able

to share a kidney, spleen, adrenal gland, appendix, nor any of your lost female organs, Nevertheless, I shall share my heart with you until death, whether mine or yours, do us apart. I love you!

Oh, yes, I dare not forget our spiritual-minded minister there at the West End Church of Christ, in Atlanta. Dr. Orpheus J. Heyward and his lovely family, Sony, Nevaeh and Nehemiah, has blessed us in a great way. I thank God for giving him the talent to study the word in such a humble manner, so as to rightly divide those truths to us. Brother O, you are so sensitive until you haven't a clue about the profound impact you have on those who hear you. You always wonder if you are touching others with the word. But, God has given you the talent to reach even teenagers, and who can reach those knuckle-heads, these days? LOL. On Sundays we don't find any sleeping teens.

And Adam McGill, the assistant minister, and his beautiful wife, Sheree, are truly an asset to the ministry. Adam, you can thank your parents for bringing you up on "drugs" in that they "drug" you to church, to Sunday school and to every mid-week class. Your God-given talent is really paying off in these uncertain days of Anti-Christ. May God keep you!

The leadership Team has proven to be great leaders of the flock as they are also led by the Holy Ghost.

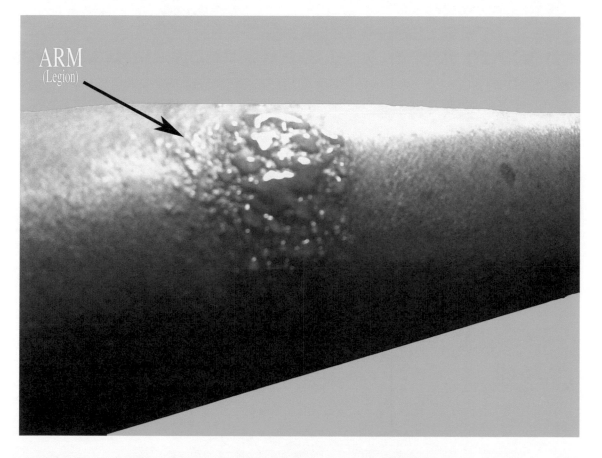

ARM
(Legion)

APPROXIMATELY TWO MONTHS AFTER THE SURGERY HAVING NO SPLEEN TO COMBAT THE INEVITABLE INFECTIONS THAT OCCURED AFTER SO MANY ORGANS WERE REMOVED.
COULD THIS BE ADRENAL FATIGUE, HAVING ONLY ONE ADRENAL GLAND TO HANDLE THE STRESS OF WRONGFULLY LOSING HER ORGANS?

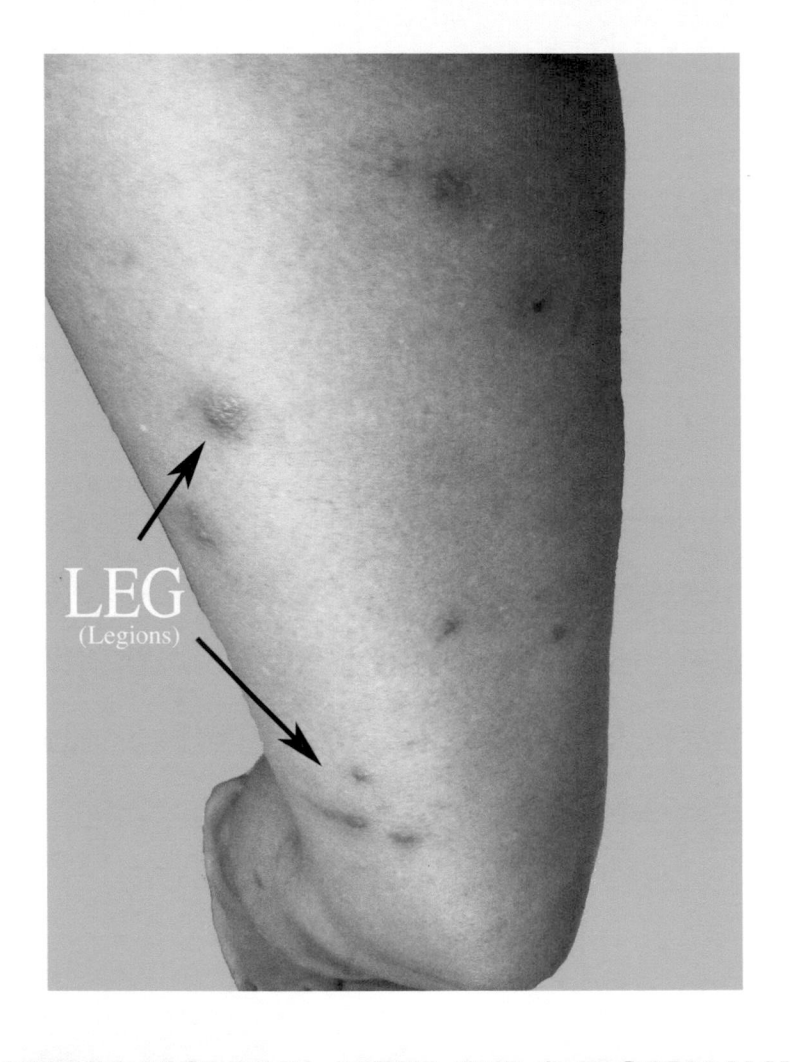

LEG
(Legions)

APPROXIMATELY THREE MONTHS AFTER THE SURGERY HAVING NO SPLEEN TO COUNTERATTACK THE INFECTIONS.

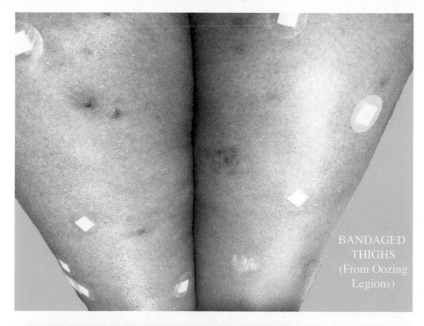

BANDAGED
THIGHS
(From Oozing
Legions)

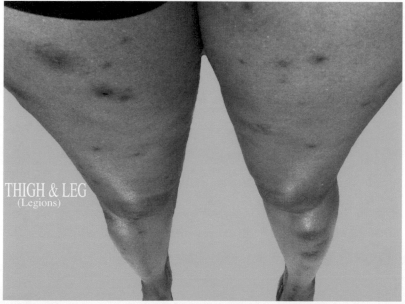

THIGH & LEG
(Legions)

TOP: OOZING LESIONS WHICH REQUIRED ANTIBOTICS AND PLENTY OF BANDAGES.
BOTTOM: FINALLY CLEARING WITH SCARRING LEFT.

LEFT KIDNEY, LEFT ADRENAL GLAND AND SPLEEN REMOVED

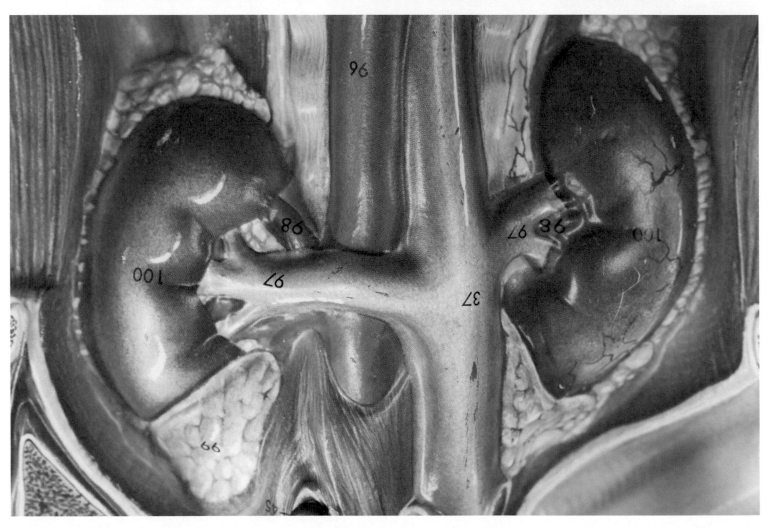

MY PERSONAL FEELINGS

EVEN HERE IN 2017, EVERY time I tell others about my surgical rape experience, they also cringe as it is also difficult for them to believe that such a botched-up situation could happen and that I was merely flipped off in a court of American law. And if those who are family can be in utter shock, then all can attest to how my family and I must despise the horrific act inflicted upon me. Were it not for my faith in God to get me through this horrible ordeal, I just don't know what would have become of me by now! I truly expected more from our justice system! It was highway robbery or should I say it was **human organ robbery!** And, as my mother have consistently said, "No doubt somebody accepted a generous bribe to fix this fight!" Maybe I should now sue the court for not seeing my illness as a personal injury crisis. But then how could the court see what was not presented to it? It was that liar, I meant, that lawyer who betrayed me to the court! And the Expert Witness (s) the other doctors for the defense should have known that removing that many healthy organs all at one time was too much for the human body. I am the victim and personal witness that my body went totally haywire as it tried to adjust to that sudden of a surgical procedure (see pictures and illustrations in this book). And my body is still in shock even after all these years. I am constantly in doctors' offices spending money I do not have, bills pilling up for tax-payers to pay from Medicaid Insurance. Then after the surgery, the removal of a healthy kidney, adrenal gland, spleen, appendix and a total hysterectomy, I suffered so many skin conditions. On those boils and lesions, I would use almost a box of band aids per week to cover the oozing from the sores. Never in my life had I any such skin condition until after the surgery. The only thing I have ever suffered was PMS, heavy periods and severe cramps. And that was only during my cycles.

After that botched surgery, I felt helpless and scared because I didn't know what was happening to my once healthy body. It really got crazy when this huge, hard growth on my face just seem to remain, no matter how hard doctors tried to cure it, it just refused to disappear. At that time, I was still working and was so embarrassed when the company let me go because of that sore and the other ones on my body. This was the second time a job had let me go due to my bodily break-outs due to my newly diagnosed Auto Immune Deficiency a couple of years after the surgery. My employers feared I had some infectious disease. Thus, in light of those embarrassing times, I seriously considered plastic surgery. But the doctor I consulted advised me not to with such a low immune system. I soon discovered that having no spleen could cause one to have a low immune system. **And I can now thank that doctor for using wisdom and not gone ahead and ill-advised me like Dr. X had just to make the money.** And God had mercy and cleared up that big, pigmented growth. And ever since the surgery I have gone through so much physical pain that I know it is by the grace of God that I am still alive today to tell my story. I am so grateful and thankful to everyone who have shown me love and compassion. I especially thank my mother and my beautiful son. They have made me feel like I am not alone and it also affect them. I am so sorry for worrying them. My family know I would never purposely harm them, but I was an innocent victim and feel very personal about it. That is why I am crying out for justice! My mother always says, "God is the greatest Judge of all and nothing is hidden from His all-seeing eyes!" Even though it is my body going through pain my family and friends have helped to relieve some of this agony with their true, loving empathy.

In my darkest moments when I become so angry about what happened, God always whisper that in spite of my challenges He is always with me through the bad times just as He also does the good times. And the reason I can be strong is because of the strength God so liberally continues to rain down.

Ever since my marriage in 2005, it quickly ended because of what my body was going through. Those unhealthy bodily changes were simply too much for my husband to take. He had married a healthy, outgoing young woman then suddenly was faced with a woman who had lost most of her internal organs. And not all of those health challenges were any fault of my own. After we finally divorced, speaking of my self-esteem, that must have divorced me too! Even after 10 years since our divorce my self-worth refuses to return. . . A man I could live without although I liked being married.

WHY REOPEN THIS CASE?

1. First of all, the Stature of Limitation prohibits legally filing another suit.
2. The case has already been taken all the way to the U.S. Supreme Court on a Pro Se, Pauperis (poor-person) basis.
3. I am no longer financially able to sustain a normal diet like most people.
4. My family nor I have the tens of thousands of dollars that my lawyer whom I feel had taken a bribe from the defense said an appeal would cost.
5. After attorney had misrepresented me, he suddenly disappeared.
6. There were so many pertinent things that the court did not see, in that my attorney refused to expose the evidence to prove Dr. X's negligence.
7. My mental and medical status and prognosis as it stands, is very dismal. I will never be well and is growing worse day by day.
8. Before the surgery my medical status was a healthy, young woman with a good job and suffered only with PMS like the majority of women do.
9. Now I have been forced to use my Social Security Insurance to modify my diet, support my illnesses and endless transportation to doctor visits on a regular basis.
10. As a result of my illness after the botched surgery, my husband could no longer bear to touch nor look at me. Thus, he finally suggested that we depart.
11. **With all these illnesses and scaring on my torso, I feel that it would be futile to expect any man to desire me as a wife. Still being so young and having my love-life taken away is simply not right! I had specifically asked Dr. X not to cut into my body and Laparoscopy was what I had seriously requested and he had agreed. Then, during the surgery, after the hysterectomy was done via Lap.**

he could not force the rest of those large organs through the Lap. So, he decided to go on and cut into my body anyway! He had no right to even bother the other healthy organs!

12. I am an only child and had plans of one day taking care of my mother. But, now I feel that she might have to be my care-giver one day. Praise God she's in good health!

13. I feel that Dr. X should not be allowed to perform surgery ever again on any human being! Maybe he should consider Veterinarian.

14. I need an honest lawyer to help prove my suspicions that Dr. X had another female patient on that same day he performed my surgery. Thus, that patient may have had an adrenal mass, which he may have confused the two of us. It's possible that he thought he was performing surgery of the other woman and mistakenly took my kidney instead. I believe he confused my kidney for her adrenal mass. It was after my surgery, and the very first and only time I had even heard of an adrenal mass being in my body. He never had told me he suspected I had an adrenal mass. So, why did he go near my kidney with that scalpel? I am so confused as to why he destroyed such healthy organs!

15. By law, it is standard procedure for a surgeon to properly prep a patient before performing a Nephrectomy to avoid complications to the patient during and after the surgery. Well, my body had not been prepared for such a major organ removal and went into total shock, causing numerous illnesses. Now I must take medications for kidney health. Plus, I never would agree to have a nephrostomy in that I never had any kidney problems.

16. I should be recompensed due to the fact that I will never be well again and my body has been totally traumatized for life. At this young age my quality of life has forcibly been taken away.

17. It needs to be proven that taking out that many organs at one time was not a wise decision on the part of a skilled surgeon. Maybe that many teeth can be pulled at once without much complications, but that is not true for internal flesh that God put there for a reason and some organs cannot be replaced like teeth.

18. It also needs to be proven that before a nephrectomy is performed, there must first be preliminary testing in order to stabilize the patient's overall system. And what are the ramifications if the patient is not properly prepped?

19. **How was it that Dr. X performed a perfect kidney extraction, but failed to realize he was handling a kidney and not just an adrenal mass, which he claimed he was taking out an adrenal mass? And, unfortunately that adrenal mass turned out to be a normal size healthy kidney!**

20. <u>**THE HOSPITAL ALSO NEEDS TO BE SUED IN THIS DEVASTATING CASE OF CHRONIC INJURY!**</u>

21. <u>**My attorney needs to be chastised for accepting a bribe and for the poor representation of me.**</u>

22. Why were there no pathology notes proving that Dr. X sent tissue samples to the lab to confirm there were cancer in the patient. This would have validated his removal of those organs. However, he sent no sample to prove he was dealing with a dangerous cancer. This case needs desperately to be reopened!

23. The reason the patient's health is worsening is because she has not been financially able to see skilled specialists. She now only has Medicare and Medicaid insurance whereas she had good insurance before she lost her job due to this abuse. This case needs to be reopened!

DEFINITIONS/MEDICAL/LEGAL TERMS

- **LAPRASCOPY SURGERY:**

When choosing Lap Surgery, the surgeon avoids having to use incisions that may leave unwanted scarring on the patient. Also, this method of performing certain types of surgery may prevent unintentional infections to the patient. This type of surgery is performed with a lighted camera at the end of a long scope, mounted with a long scope, mounted with a lighted camera at the end to guide the doctor to the exact area of tissue that is in question. In most cases, a tiny incision, approximately 2-3 inches in length is made into the patient's flesh, which requires only about 6-8 sutures. In some cases, surgery staples can substitute for sewing in stiches.

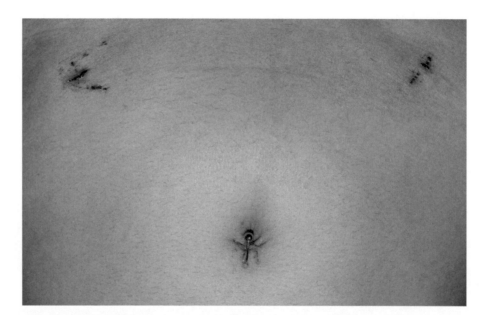

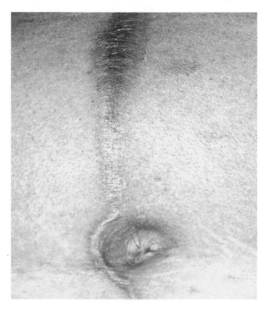

Traditional surgery done on MzAnn, and this scarring is the result.

- **STANDARD OF CARE, FIDUCIARY**

watchfulness, attention, caution and prudence that a reasonable person in the circumstances would exercise. If a person's actions do not meet this standard of care, then their act fail to meet the duty of care which all people (supposedly) have toward others. Failure to meet the standard is negligence, and any damages resulting therefrom may be claimed in a lawsuit by the injured party. The problem is that the "standard" is often a subjective issue upon which reasonable people can differ. A treatment process that a clinician should follow for a certain type of patient, illness, or clinical circumstance.

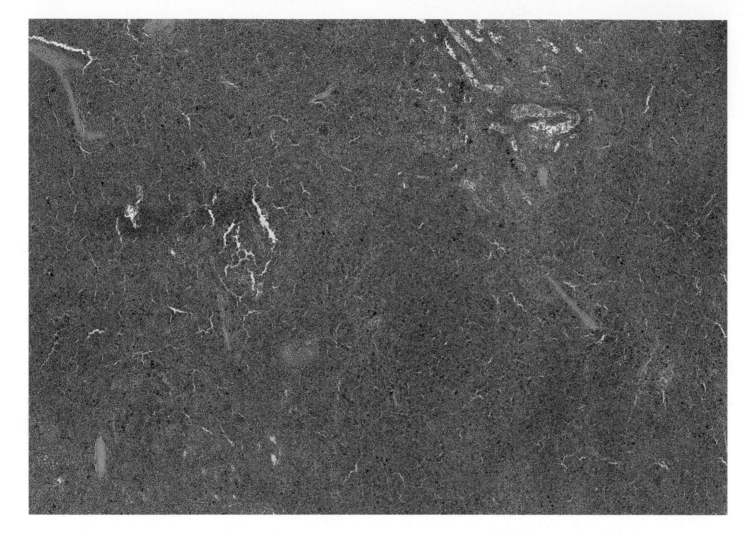

CANCER UNDER MICROSCOPE/BUT PATIENT NEVER HAD CANCER!

- **TRANSCRIPT:**

A copy and permanent record by Law. A written record of spoken language in court proceedings

- *Pro se* **legal representation**, Filing appeals on behalf of themselves, which basically means advocating on one's own behalf before a court, rather than being represented by a lawyer. This may occur in court proceeding, whether one is the plaintiff in a civil case. *Pro-se* is a Latin phase meaning "for oneself" or "on one's own behalf".

- <u>**LEGAL GROUNDS:**</u>

During my Pro Se appeals, I had taken those appeals all the way to the U.S. Supreme Court through Writ of Certiorari. However, I never discovered a sensible definition for the law term, Legal Grounds. Only the appeals courts, kept replying that I must include legal grounds with the Writ.

- <u>**STATURE OF LIMITATION:**</u>

A space in which the time has expired to consult an attorney for the purpose of attempting to obtain justice in your case.

UNLAWFUL ACTIONS BY ATTORNEY

1. During the three-day trial in 2010, my lawyer, the one I had actually hired, had not prepared me well at all! Then he hired a younger lawyer to defend me in court. On the day of court, the one I hired astonished me when he quickly tried to rush and get me prepared with a list of things I should do and say when called to the stand. There was specifically one question I never will forget. I was coyly asked by the defending attorney if I had ever sued anyone before. Now, I know that was a tactic to make it seem as though I had a habit of conveniently suing. The suit he had referred to was a car accident of which I was not at fault. This was another point where my attorney should have objected or at least let me explain the pain and suffering I had endured from that car accident and as a result had been deemed medically incapacitated in that the other driver was at fault.

2. At the beginning of the trial my attorney tried to prepare me with some more confusing questions and handed them to me at the last minute. I was already foggy from being so ill from the surgery that my mind became even more cloudy. It was just too much for me to process in a sane fashion. Too many unbelievable things had happened!

3. Then, back in my seat, whenever I nodded my head in agreeance with my Expert Witness, my attorney had seen fit to advise me not to nod like that. I guess he didn't want the jury to see me agree for fear they might be persuaded my way. Well it is all making sense now. The treatment I received from my lawyer was apparently all a part of his game-plan to sell out the case.

4. Whenever I felt well enough I did some teacher substituting. So, one day I met another teacher who wisely informed me of something, after I had told her my unjust plight. At the time I was feeling I might never get justice then she said, "Sometimes justice takes a long time!" Now I know that God moved her

to say that, in that my hope was waning very fast. Now I know that justice will prevail through my Father in Heaven. I pray that God will forgive my momentarily lack of faith. It was just that I had suffered for so long and cried so many tears that my flesh had become weak. One never knows who God may place in one's path at the right time. He had sent her to me which caused me to examine my faith in Him.

5. Another weird thing had happened to prove that my attorney had set me up for the fall. I did not understand why, in his office one day before the trial, he had advised me that when we went to court, I was to dress like I was going to a fashion show. I vividly recall those were the exact words he said to me! Now I realize this was another part of his devious game. Also, on the day of the trial my attorney alerted me that Medical Malpractice cases were hardly won by the patient. Then why had he, after handling my case for two years, decide to tell me on the day of court? Then suddenly on court day he had matter-of-fact informed me that the Debbie Downer News had just reported those Malpractice statistics. But for 2 years he had made me feel as though my case was a sure winner. To this very day this careless act that I once called a mistake was an intentionally careless act towards me and I went from sad to mad when I thought about how he bamboozled me!!

6. Also, why did my lawyer not summon the pathologist who received my healthy organs in her lab? She would have given her account of the conversation she had with Doctor X when she surprisingly informed him that a kidney was in the bag that she had not expected to receive. What a grievous injustice I suffered!!!

7. After he had lost the case for me and I was in a total state of shock, as my family, my attorney and I headed to the parking lot, he matter-of fact, informed, "You could have polled the jurors, you know." I glared daggers at him. "No, I did not and what does poll mean?" Then he simply said, "you could have asked them who was for you and who were against you." I knew that if I had asked why he was just now letting me know that, I probably would have said some things a Christian should not say.

CASES/ORGANIZATIONS THAT FIGHTS FOR JUSTICE

HERE IS SOME MEDICAL MALPRACTICE cases and organization that was also horrific but those patients received some kind of justice. Their injuries were seriously considered and treated fairly in a court of American law. So, I ask why did I not receive a fair trial for the doctor having made the mistake of removing all my healthy organs? The Center for Justice and Accountability is for human rights which mine have also been taken away!

PATIENTS WHO RECEIVED JUSTICE, I DID NOT! (EXCEPT FOR ONE)

PLEASE READ NOW!!!

See: www.bostonglobe.com Title: Hospital Removes Patient's Kidney by Accident. After a surgeon, mistakenly removed this patient's healthy kidney, she was given another kidney. The hospital was sued for the doctor's mistake.

See: www.dailymail.com Title: You're Taking Out the Wrong Kidney, Surgeon Was Told. A student who was watching the surgery, warned the surgeon he was taking out the wrong kidney, but he ignored her. Several weeks later, the patient died. This was an unfortunate situation, but at least this case received some recognition. Absurdly, my healthy kidney removal was treated with the utmost disregard!! Center for Justice and Accountability www.center4justice.org. This is a Human Rights organization where cases concerning human injustice can be found. In our case, we can go here to place membership to have our need for changing the unfair medical malpractice whose laws favor doctors over patients.

COPY AND PASTE WWW.NEWSER.COM. THEN SEARCH FOR, HOSPITAL REMOVES WRONG KIDNEY.

POST REMARKS

NOW THAT YOU ALL HAVE read my distressful, unbelievable story you can make your decision to either help me or take Dr. X's side. Nevertheless, it is my family and my prayers that you will decide to reach out with any legal assistance you can. I am pressed that there are so many issues in this case that needs to be revealed by having a completely new trial. But, every word I have written in this booklet is the truth! And my family and I will not have peace of mind until I get justice. So, I honestly ask what if your loved one had this kind of thing happen? Wouldn't you be just as adamant about bringing their offender (s) to justice? My opinion is that you would be on the case as well. However, you may have the funds to hire an attorney to file appeals along with the **legal grounds t**o substantiate their claim and not have to settle for a Pro Se appeal (see definitions) like I had. And during our laymen appeals we had not an inkling of an idea of how to search for the documents made available at the Courthouse. So, the **legal grounds** documents made no sense to us at all, but we did what we could to discover a few cases. In other words, we were forced to sink or swim. . . sadly we sank for the time being. Now through our faith in the Almighty we have resumed to seek justice from those of you out there who know the law and can find some **legal ground**s for this case. God help us to find those attorneys who will fight with us to finally get justice! We thank God for allowing us to realize that sometimes justice takes a long time and the faithful will eventually get it through God's strength!

God has truly, through my physical issues, allowed my body to fight against the constant attacks on it. Though I struggle daily because of the gruesome attack by Dr. X, I feel that God have decided that I won't be defeated. I'm asking for justice by our so-called justice system that had all the evidence that Dr. X breached the Standard of Care. I pray that Dr. X soon realizes that he owes me because I trusted him while I lay helpless under his care. Dr. X you have caused me to live a life of deep financial difficulties. I now live in public housing, way below the poverty level, because I haven't been able to work. You have gone on with your life as though what you did was alright. No! Do the right thing now, Dr. X! Do you recall how, by your own admission you whispered to me in court that you thought you were doing the right thing? You admitted your mistake so it's only fair that you give me the justice. Put me back in the position I was in before you gutted me! I know you cannot replace those organs, but you can relieve my mental stress by making my heart lighter towards you and the system. Nevertheless, my spirit is very much alive and won't rest on this earth knowing the wrong I received by such skilled hands. Surely my spirit will rest in heaven but yours is in jeopardy unless you right your, wrong.

PS: God please forgive me if I'm wrong about this whole situation. God, you said that I shouldn't be afraid of them that can kill merely the body but rather that I should fear You who is able to kill both body and SOUL. Lord I'm asking for another opportunity to tell my side of this ordeal in court! In the name of my Savior, Jesus, The Christ!! And thank you, Father for giving me a potion of daily bread in the form of the word in 2 Timothy 1: 7, "God had not given us the spirit of fear, but of power and of love and of a sound mind." I refuse to let man have my mind. Not even you and your sidekicks, Dr. X!

ABOUT THE AUTHOR

MZANN WAS BORN ON CHRISTMAS Day. She has one son. She has been a Christian for 30 plus years, where she also graduated from Southwestern Christian College and received a degree in Computer Science which afforded her to work as a Computer Operator for Home Depot, a Software Analyst for Matria Healthcare and as a Voter Registration TS Troubleshooter. She freelanced as a Court Researcher and later because of 15 years as an educator, she retired and began working on a second degree at the local University but in the last quarter she was hindered due to her lack of funding. She is now tutoring children along with her special homeschooled, Lulu. Presently she volunteers as the Vice President in her community on the Residence Association Committee. There, her vision is to unite all residents into one place, on one accord. MzAnn loves her community, friends and especially her family.

Her book is written with hopes that those who read it may find encouragement and strength through any life barriers and life-altering events they may be encountering. She thanks God for bringing her to this place and time to see this book published. She did not think she would even live long enough to see its fruits. Her sincere praises go to GOD only!!!!

She extends a BIG thanks to her wonderful mother for taking her many phone notes and formatting them into this book, which she never could have done it without her mother's author-expertise.

LEGAL REFERENCES PROVIDED IN THIS BOOK

THE SNAPSHOTS OF PATIENT'S SORES and boils is the true after-effect of what she looked like as a result of the ill treatment from her surgeon having removed several healthy organs. These break-outs had never happened to her before the surgery but along with many other illnesses, she still has these sporadic skin problems.

The Idol called

1999-2018 by SHB

A letter from the idol called Santa Claus.

Dear People of the world:

It was one cold and snowy day
When upon my cozy bed I lay.
I was about to cut a snore,
When, a man in white walked right through my closed door.
I glanced at the window and outside it suddenly was night.
I trembled profusely through fear and affright.
Then jumping from the bed, I threw on my Santa suit,
And was about to tie up my boot.
But the man in white motioned with his hand.
He said, "Have no fear, Dear Man."
I wondered what manner of man this was who spoke.
And much calmer now slowly I took off my coat.
The man in white proceeded to inform why he came.
He said, "Tell me Dear Man, what is your name?"
Sticking out my chest, I replied, "My name is Santa Claus.
Everyone knows that. . .
Can't you tell by my red suit and hat!?"
Then the man in white pointed an accusing finger at me,
"Don't you know that people worship you!?
Do you not know that God made you merely human too?
God created the trees from whence came your suit.
God even made the animals from whence came your boots."
With wide eyes, I cried, "But I only intend to spread Christmas cheer!
I love it when children call me Santa Dear!"
Then the man in white sadly sighed,
"That's exactly what I was sent to warn you about.

You allow little children to think of you as the Almighty God, no doubt!
But in six days, the world and man God did wove.
And it displeases Him when you get the glory for which He strove!"
Then I began to scratch my beard in puzzlement, and said,
"I never looked at it quite that way.
I never meant to lead God's people astray!
What can I do? It's too late to stop now?
The children do worship me . . . they even pray and bow!"
The man in white simply smiled and, said, "There is something you can do Dear Man.
You can reach people all over this land.
Just tell them that you've cheated the God of heaven, and that you repent!
To tell you this is why I was sent."
Then reluctantly, I cried, "But that would disillusion all children to be so bold!"
The man in white said, "Well, wouldn't you rather disappoint them now,
Than to have them later lose their soul?"
I pondered on that while the man in white stood patiently by.
Then, with sincere remorse, I blurted, "I want to repent before I die!"
I awakened myself when I screamed.
Only to realize it had been a ghastly dream.
I looked all around and the man in white was suddenly gone.
But deep within, I had a creepy feeling I wasn't alone.
So, People, immediately I sat down to write this letter to you,
So, you'll know Santa Claus not to be true.
I'm just a mere mortal in a red and white suit
And who wears a pair of shiny long black boots.
Though, the name Santa has a nice ring.
It can't take the place of God Almighty, for He is the giver of all good things!
And if any of you've also given Santa Claus the glory,
Please stop to consider this dreadful story!

Exodus 20:3-- THOU SHALL HAVE NO OTHER gods BEFORE ME!

Acts 15:20--ABSTAIN FROM THE POLUTION OF IDOLS!

<u>WEDDING DINNER INVITATION</u>

©2008-2018 by SHB

MATTHEW 22: 1-14 ©1998-2017 Note: Best understood when read with 2 Peter 1: 5-7 (CHRISTIAN ATTRIBUTES).

Our heavenly Father bids: All things are ready, come to the feast!

He has prepared _FAITH_ salad, _VIRTURE_ rolls, not to say the least.

There will be _KNOWLEDGE_ loaf dipped in _TEMPERANCE_ fondue.

The savory taste of _PATIENCE_ stew was whipped up just for you.

You'll sniff the alluring aroma from the roast of _GODLINESS._

And, by the way! The _BROTHERLY-KINDNESS_ greens are simply the best!

And last, but certainly not least, the desert of which you all shall get a generous taste. . .

A thick slice of _LOVE_ pie you just cannot afford to waste.

The groom will be Jesus, seated at the Father's right hand.

And, of course, the Holy Ghost will be Jesus' Best Man.

The bride, Christ's church, will be lovely, all garbed in holiness.

So, the Father bids all, Come, be my honored guests!

BLITE

One of my parents is Black. The other parent is White.

Does that make me Black, White, or maybe Blite?

Most of my peers have a single race they can hold true.

I can't make just one heritage claim, I'm not like you.

I used to get angry when others taunted me with names.

But now I only pity them for taking a role in life's sick games.

Some people can be cruel with their race supremacy syndromes.

But as for me, living with both parents is like living in a heavenly home.

My mother often tells me she loves me. My father tells me to just be strong.

Because some people would make me feel that being Blite is wrong.

My peers sometimes expect me to take sides.

But I refuse to, because in both my heritages I take awesome pride!

DAYDREAMS

Until you, time for me was an endless and useless process.

My daydreams were shallow, my arms found no warmth in anyone else's caress.

My days were filled with idleness of thought.

Now my daydreams, with wonders, you have taught.

If I could double the hours in a day.

In my daydreams you'd still stay.

Kiss me, my love, your sweet breath on my face.

Make me daydream of roses, wine and lace.

Take my hand and lead me to that place of "No Hate."

There daydreaming of you would be my fate.

If reincarnation were real to me.

I daydream of what I'd like to be . . .

A sturdy old oak tree.

I'd want you to be the soil in which I stand.

So, that I could daydream of you a thousand years upon God's green land.

Your presence in my life has inspired my daily duties.

Just to daydream of you fills me with breathtakingly beauty.

My love, don't stray too far from my mental vibes.

Let me keep this daydream warm, wonderful and alive.

If you were my daydream but for one day,

I'd still thank God for that, and to Him I'd always pray.

Come, let me share your innermost daydreams from time to time.

Who knows? Your daydreams just may equate with mine.

TIME

Time . . . the space of an endless process.

A concept no mere man can possess.

The astute have struggled to monopolize it.

But only to become even more, baffled by it.

Time is like the wind we know not its origin.

We know not even where it begins.

And only God knows where it ends.

Time has no birthdays to joy, nor funerals to mourn.

Time creates a thin line between night and dawn.

Time's evasiveness causes some to marvel.

Still time's sluggishness causes others to quarrel.

Time is a concept all have in common.

Man, beast, the trees, the rivers and even the Orion.

I wonder about Time, yet never burdened down.

My mind stayed on Jesus, I'm heaven bound.

When in heaven I'll laugh in Time's face.

For God has declared that to Him, a thousand years is as but one day (2 peter 3:8).

SHB © 1998-2018

HOW TO BECOME A CHRISTIAN

1. Hear the gospel-Romans 10: 17 "Faith comes by hearing".
2. Believe what is heard-Hebrews 11:6- "For without faith it is impossible to please God".
3. Repent of sins (Acts 2: 38), "Repent of your sins, everyone, of you!"
4. Confess Christ (Matt. 10:32) "Whosoever shall confess me before men, I will confess him before my Father".
5. Be baptized (Acts 2: 38) "And be baptized everyone, of you for the remission of your sins and you will receive the gift of the Holy Ghost".
6. And the Lord adds to the church-Acts 2: 47-And the Lord added to the church daily as many as should be saved."

You are invited to visit a Church of Christ nearest you and watch the West End CofC on YouTube, with Brother, Doctor Orpheus J. Heyward.

Printed in the United States
By Bookmasters